Lift Up Your
Heart

WALNUT SPRINGS PRESS

Although we live in
increasingly perilous times,
the Lord LOVES US
and is mindful of us.
He is ALWAYS ON OUR SIDE
as we do what is right.
He will HELP US
in time of need.

Thomas S. Monson

I do believe that the way we

react to adversity

can be a major factor in how

happy and successful

we can be in life.

If we approach adversities wisely,

our hardest times can be times of

greatest growth,

which in turn can lead toward times of

greatest happiness.

JOSEPH B. WIRTHLIN

[T]his brief time away from our heavenly home and parents is a time when we are given our agency for the purpose of being tried and tested in every way (see 2 Nephi 2:24–28). You should expect some "down" days and some hard tests. Learn from them. Grow from them. Be stronger because of them.

Ardeth G. Kapp

As you keep moving forward,

you can stay upright

even when outside forces

try to pull you down.

Bonnie L. Oscarson

I love those who can SMILE in trouble, who can GATHER STRENGTH from distress, and GROW BRAVE by reflection. 'Tis the business of little minds to shrink, but they whose HEART IS FIRM, and whose conscience approves their conduct, will pursue their PRINCIPLES unto death.

Leonardo da Vinci

All that we suffer and all
that we endure, especially if
we endure it patiently, builds up
our character, purifies our hearts,
expands our souls, and makes us
more tender and charitable,
more worthy to be called
the children of God.

Orson F. Whitney

We are troubled on every

side, yet NOT DISTRESSED;

we are perplexed,

but NOT IN DESPAIR;

Persecuted,

but NOT FORSAKEN;

cast down,

but NOT DESTROYED.

2 Corinthians 4:8–9

The past is behind—

LEARN from it;

the future is ahead—

PREPARE for it;

the present is here—

LIVE in it.

Thomas S. Monson

To become a winner in the race for eternal life requires effort—constant work, striving, and enduring well with God's help. But the key is that we must take it just one step at a time. . . . Greatness is best measured by how well an individual responds to the happenings in life that appear to be totally unfair, unreasonable, and undeserved. . . . Day by day we can make the effort to gain the power to last and to suffer without yielding.

Marvin J. Ashton

The story of our search for happiness is written in such a way that if we continue to trust in God and follow His commandments through the challenging times, even those times will bring us closer to the happiness we are seeking.

Coleen K. Menlove

The Saints will be put to

tests that will

TRY THE INTEGRITY

of the best of them.

The pressure

will become so great

that the more righteous

among them will

CRY UNTO THE LORD

day and night until

deliverance comes.

Heber C. Kimball

Every *adversity*,

every *failure*,

every *heartache*

carries with it the seed of an

equal or greater benefit.

NAPOLEON HILL

Our faith in Jesus Christ enables
us to meet any challenge.
We, in fact, often find our faith
deepened and our relationship
with Heavenly Father and His Son
refined in adversity.

Carole M. Stephens

No pain will last forever. It is not easy, but life was never meant to be either easy or fair. Repentance and the lasting hope that forgiveness brings will always be worth the effort.

Boyd K. Packer

Come unto me, all ye that labour
and are heavy laden,
and I will give you rest.

Take my yoke upon you,
and learn of me;
for I am meek and lowly in heart:
and ye shall find
rest unto your souls.

Matthew 11:28–29

I thank the Lord

that I may have

passed some of the tests,

but maybe there

will have to be

MORE

before I shall have

been polished to do

ALL

that the Lord

would have me do.

Harold B. Lee

No difficulty can discourage, no obstacle dismay, no trouble dishearten the [woman] who has acquired the art of being alive. Difficulties are but dares of fate, obstacles but hurdles to try [her] skill, troubles but bitter tonics to give [her] strength; and [she] rises higher and looms greater after each encounter with adversity.

Ella Wheeler Wilcox

It matters not what may befall,
What threat'ning hand hangs over me;
He is my rampart through it all,
My refuge from mine enemy.

Come unto him all ye depressed,
Ye erring souls whose eyes are dim,
Ye weary ones who long for rest
Come unto him! Come unto him!

from the hymn "Come unto Him"

If I were asked to give what I consider

the single most useful bit of advice

for all humanity, it would be this:

Expect trouble

as an inevitable part of life,

and when it comes,

hold your head high,

look it squarely in eye and say,

"I will be bigger than you.

YOU CANNOT DEFEAT ME."

Ann Landers

Our past and present sufferings cannot, as Paul said, "be compared with the glory which shall be revealed in us" (Romans 8:18) in the eternities. "For after much tribulation come the blessings. Wherefore the day cometh that ye shall be crowned with much glory" (D&C 58:4).

So tribulation is useful in the sense that it is helpful to get into the celestial kingdom. . . .

In our time we are going through an increasingly difficult time of refining and testing. The tests are more subtle because the lines between good and evil are being eroded. Very little seems to be sacred in any of our public communication. In this environment we will need to make sure where we stand all of the time in our commitment to eternal truths and covenants.

JAMES E. FAUST

Even in our most diligent efforts to live the gospel, all of us will make mistakes, and all of us will sin. What a comforting assurance it is to know that through our Savior's redeeming sacrifice, we can be forgiven and made clean again.

Ann M. Dibb

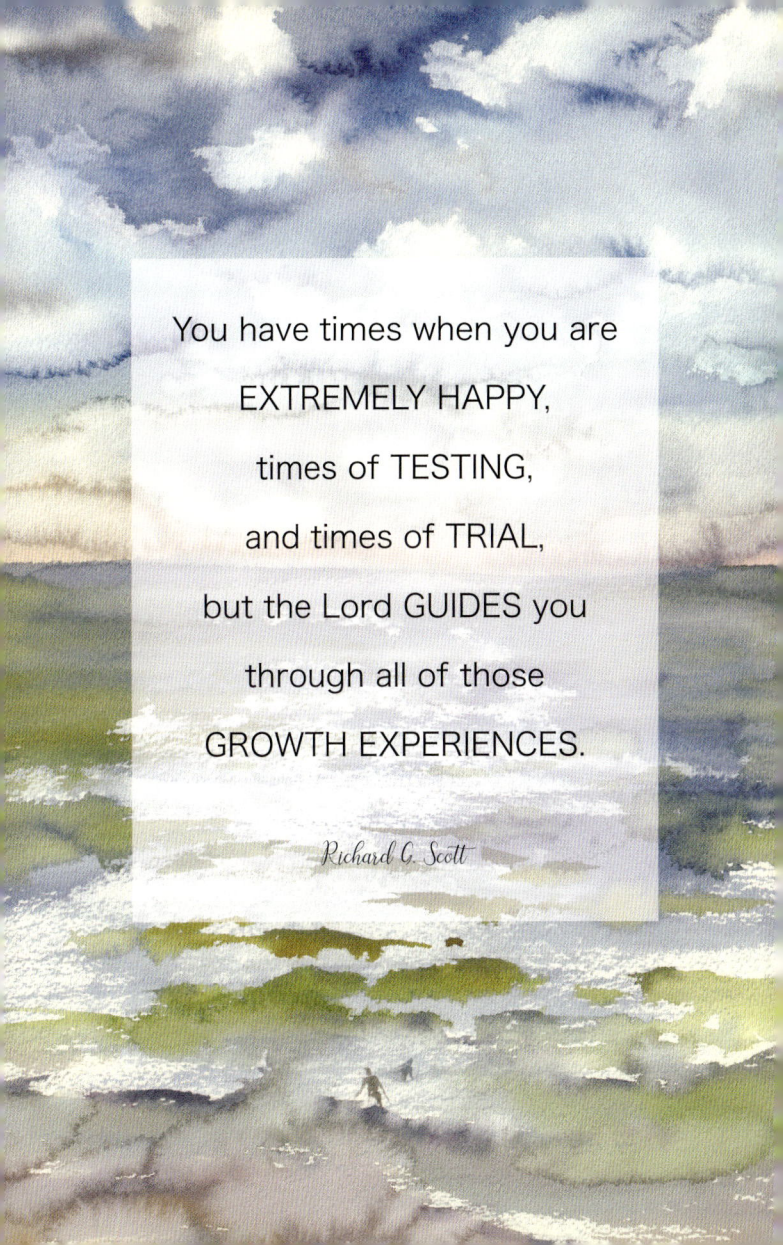

You have times when you are

EXTREMELY HAPPY,

times of TESTING,

and times of TRIAL,

but the Lord GUIDES you

through all of those

GROWTH EXPERIENCES.

Richard G. Scott

Rejoicing in hope;
patient in tribulation;
continuing instant in prayer;

Bless them which persecute you:
bless, and curse not.

Rejoice with them that do rejoice,
and weep with them that weep.

Be of the same mind one toward another.

ROMANS 12:12, 14–17

We truly need Him

every hour,

whether they be hours of

sunshine or of rain.

Thomas S. Monson

I do not know why we have the many trials that we have, but it is my personal feeling that the reward is so great, so eternal and everlasting, so joyful and beyond our understanding that in that day of reward, we may feel to say to our merciful, loving Father, "Was that all that was required?" I believe that if we could daily remember and recognize the depth of that love our Heavenly Father and our Savior have for us, we would be willing to do anything to be back in Their presence again, surrounded by Their love eternally. What will it matter, dear sisters, what we suffered here if, in the end, those trials are the very things which qualify us for eternal life and exaltation in the kingdom of God with our Father and Savior?

Linda S. Reeves

Happiness does not depend on

what happens *outside* of you

but on what happens

inside of you;

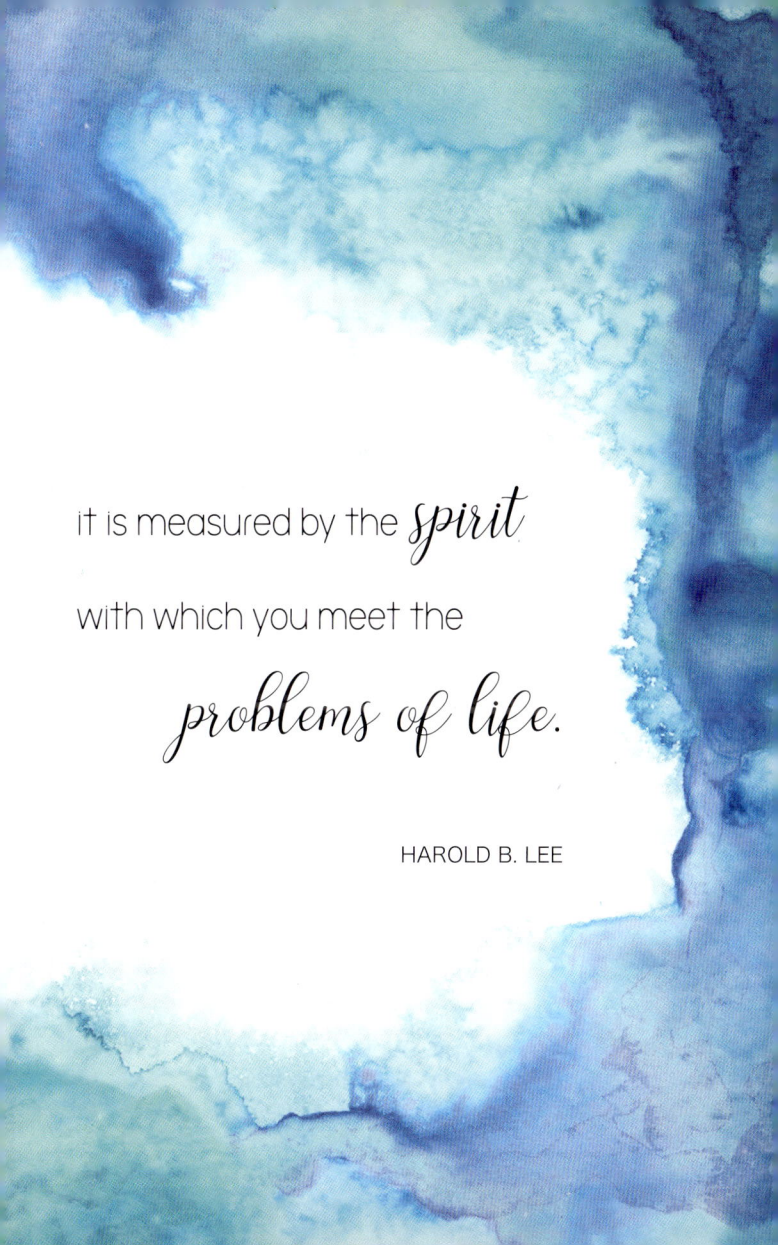

it is measured by the *spirit*

with which you meet the

problems of life.

HAROLD B. LEE

I will go forward . . . I will smile at the rage of the tempest, and ride fearlessly and triumphantly across the boisterous ocean of circumstance. . . . And the "testimony of Jesus" will light up a lamp that will guide my vision through the portals of immortality, and communicate to my understanding the glories of the celestial kingdom.

Eliza R. Snow

Difficulties come into our lives, problems we do not anticipate and which we would never choose. None of us is immune. The purpose of mortality is to learn and to grow to be more like our Father, and it is often during the difficult times that we learn the most, as painful as the lessons may be. Our lives can also be filled with joy as we follow the teachings of the gospel of Jesus Christ.

Thomas S. Monson

If we lock ourselves in

a prison of failure and self-pity,

we are the only jailers …

we have the only key

to our freedom.

Og Mandino

If you have stumbled

or even been

lost for a time,

you can

move forward with faith

and not wander to and fro

in the world any longer.

There are those who stand ready

to guide you back

to peace and security.

BOYD K. PACKER

Mercies and blessings come in different forms—sometimes as hard things. Yet the Lord said, "Thou shalt thank the Lord thy God in ALL things" (D&C 59:7; emphasis added). ALL THINGS means just that: good things, difficult things—not just some things. He has commanded us to be grateful because He knows being grateful will make us happy. This is another evidence of His love.

Bonnie D. Parkin

Evil will always be with us in this world. Part of mortality's great test is to be in the world without becoming like the world. In His Intercessory Prayer, the Savior asked His Heavenly Father, "I pray not that thou shouldest take them out of the world, but that thou shouldest keep them from the evil" (John 17:15). But even as the Savior warned of persecution, He promised peace: "Peace I leave with you, my peace I give unto you. . . . Let not your heart be troubled, neither let it be afraid" (John 14:27).

Robert D. Hales

Just as we develop
our physical muscles
through overcoming opposition—
such as lifting weights—
we develop
our character muscles
by overcoming challenges
and adversity.

Stephen R. Covey

Our Heavenly Father did not put us on earth to fail but to SUCCEED GLORIOUSLY.

Richard G. Scott

If pain and sorrow and total punishment immediately followed the doing of evil, no soul would repeat a misdeed. If joy and peace and rewards were instantaneously given the doer of good, there could be no evil—all would do good and not because of the rightness of doing good. There would be no test of strength, no development of character, no growth of powers, no free agency. . . . There would also be an absence of joy, success, resurrection, eternal life, and godhood.

Spencer W. Kimball

Every

trial and experience

you have passed through

is *necessary*

for your salvation.

Brigham Young

Difficult roads often lead
to beautiful destinations.
The best is yet to come.

Zig Ziglar

When thou art in

tribulation,

and all these things

are come upon thee . . .

if thou turn to

the Lord thy God,

and shalt be obedient

unto his voice;

(For the Lord thy God

is a merciful God;)

he will not forsake thee.

Deuteronomy 4:30–31

${T}$he only way
to get through life is to

LAUGH

your way through it.
You either have to laugh or cry.
I prefer to laugh.
Crying gives me a headache.

Marjorie Pay Hinckley

Why does the Lord allow
suffering and adversity
to come to us in this life?
Simply put, it is part of
the plan for our growth
and progress—
we "shouted for joy"
(Job 38:7) when we knew
we would have the opportunity
to come to earth
to experience mortality.

Linda K. Burton

No PERSON CAN BECOME STRONG
WITHOUT STRUGGLE, WITHOUT THE
EFFORT OF PITTING [HERSELF] AGAINST
TROUBLE AND HARDSHIP. AND TO
MEET AND DEAL WITH LIFE CREATIVELY
WE WILL ALWAYS NEED TO BE ALERT
AND THOUGHTFUL AND TO THINK IN
A POSITIVE MANNER, CONSTANTLY
RALLYING PERSONALITY FORCES INTO
EFFECTIVE AND DESIRABLE ACTION.

Norman Vincent Peale

Character cannot be developed

in ease and quiet.

Only through experience

of trial and suffering

can the soul be strengthened,

ambition inspired,

and success achieved.

HELEN KELLER

We have to prepare even for
what we are unprepared for and
DO THE BEST WE CAN . . .
to improve, to repent, to be grateful
for all that is good—
and to HAVE FAITH AND HOPE
even [in hard times] . . . .
And whatever happens in the interim,
there is solid assurance that
LIFE IS EVERLASTING,
and that eternal progress
is its purpose.

Richard L. Evans

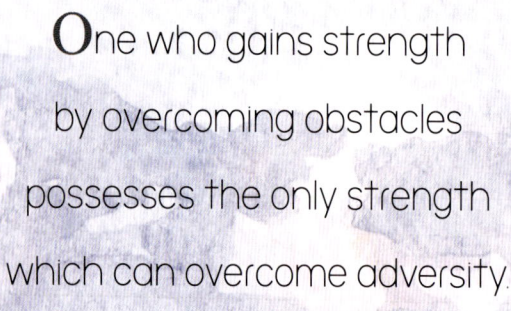

One who gains strength

by overcoming obstacles

possesses the only strength

which can overcome adversity.

Albert Schweitzer

Here, then, is a great truth. In the pain, in the agony, and the heroic endeavors of life, we pass through a REFINER'S FIRE, and the insignificant and the unimportant in our lives can MELT AWAY like dross and make our faith BRIGHT, INTACT, and STRONG.

James E. Faust

Let

God's promises

shine on your

problems.

Corrie ten Boom

God will give us priceless, personal assurances through the Holy Ghost . . . Whether in tranquil or turbulent times, our best source of comfort is the Comforter. . . .

Regarding trials, including of our faith and patience, there are no exemptions—only variations.

NEAL A. MAXWELL

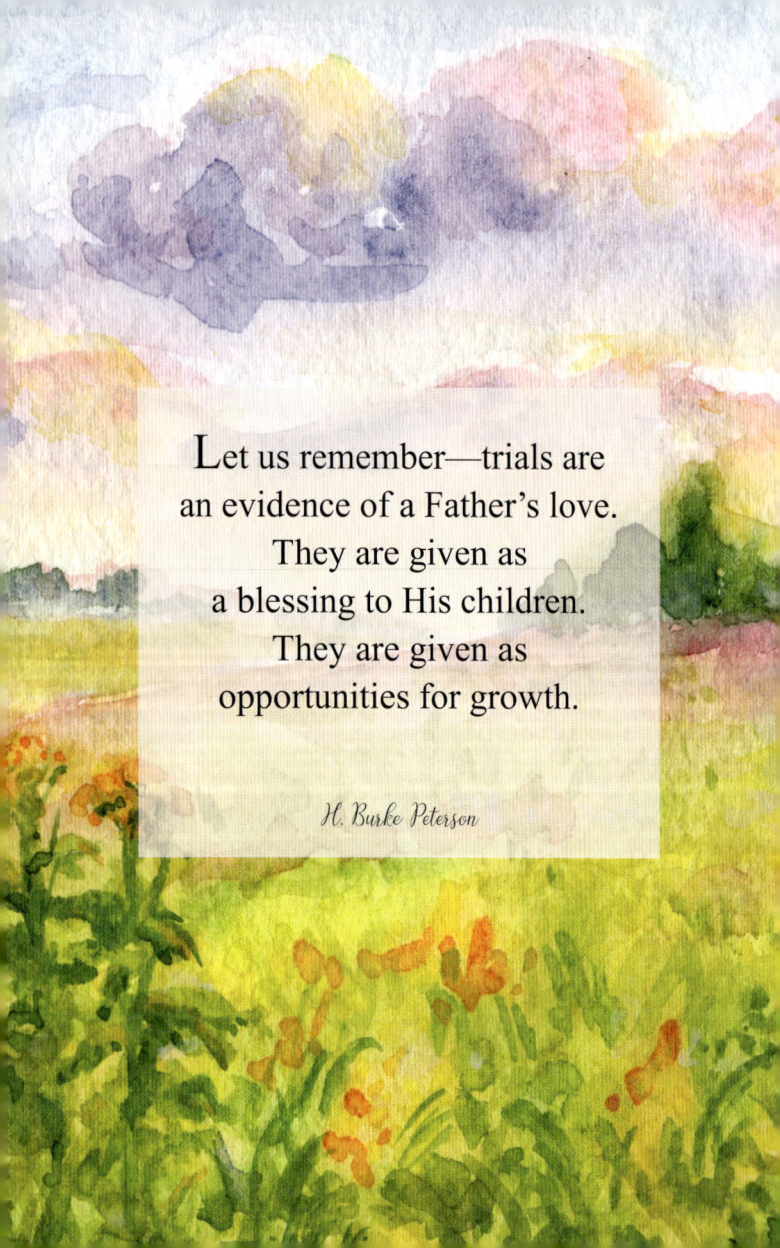

Let us remember—trials are
an evidence of a Father's love.
They are given as
a blessing to His children.
They are given as
opportunities for growth.

H. Burke Peterson

Knowing that we can trust God and our Savior completely is one of the greatest gifts we have been given. In the scriptures, the Savior admonished us, "Consider the lilies of the field, how they grow; they toil not, neither do they spin" (Matthew 6:28). He also taught, "Seek ye first the kingdom of God, and his righteousness; and all these things shall be added unto you" (Matthew 6:33). I love these comforting scriptures, which remind me to focus on the important aspects of life.

Donna Moyer

God hath said
that He would have
a tried people,
that He would
purge them as gold.

Joseph Smith

To explain a trial would be to destroy
its object, which is that of calling forth
simple faith and implicit obedience.
If we knew why the Lord sent us this
or that trial, it would thereby cease to
be a trial either of faith or of patience.

Alfred Edersheim

Knowing that eventually all things will work together for our good will help us endure affliction like the faithful people from the scriptures who knew of [the Father's] promises and trusted in them, "having seen them afar off, and were persuaded of them, and embraced them" (Hebrews 11:13). We too can embrace this promise. . . . While it may be true in some instances that our promised blessings will be fulfilled only in the eternities, it is also true that as we search, pray, and believe, we will often recognize things working together for our good in this life.

Susan W. Tanner

It was meant to be that life would be a challenge. To suffer some anxiety, some depression, some disappointment, even some failure is normal. . . . [I]f [you] have a good, miserable day once in a while, or several in a row, . . . stand steady and face them. Things will straighten out. There is great purpose in our struggle in life.

Boyd K. Packer

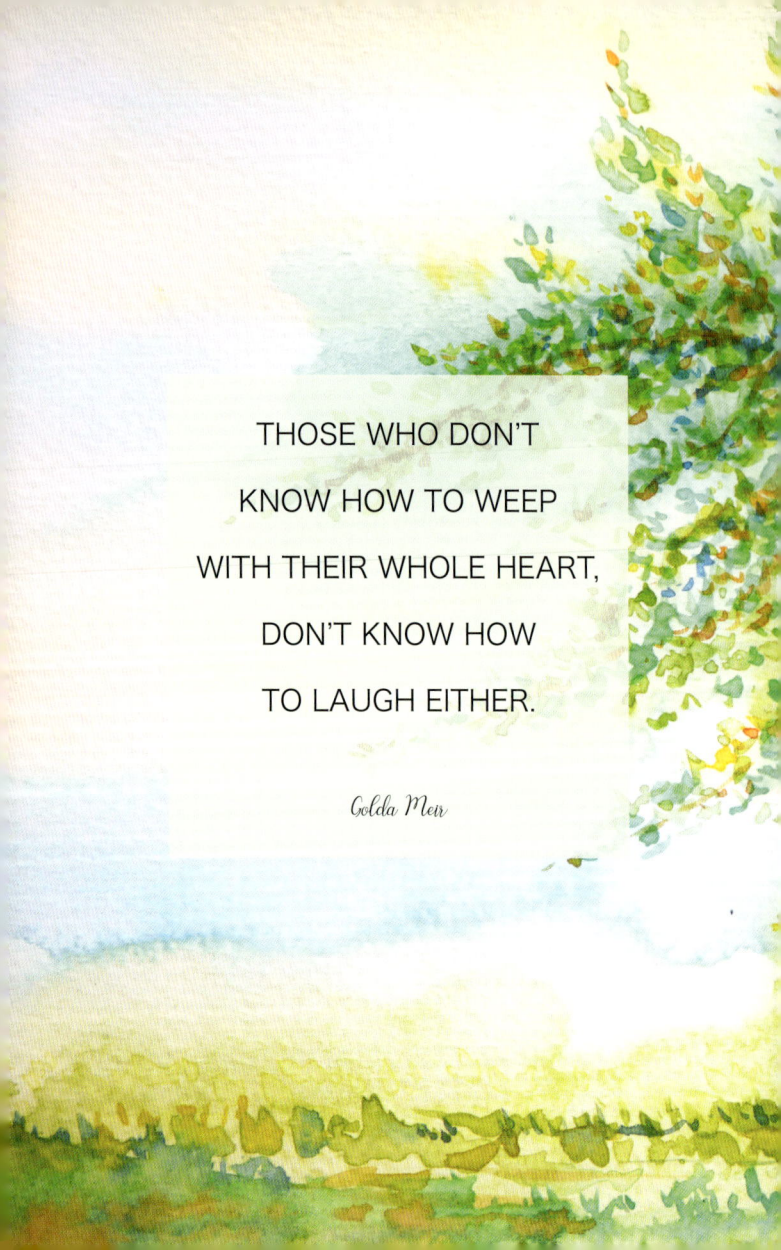

THOSE WHO DON'T
KNOW HOW TO WEEP
WITH THEIR WHOLE HEART,
DON'T KNOW HOW
TO LAUGH EITHER.

Golda Meir

Our task is to become our
best selves. One of God's
greatest gifts to us
is the joy of trying again,
for no failure
ever need be final.

Thomas S. Monson

Sometimes we spend so much time trying to determine what we did wrong in the past to deserve the unpleasant happenings of the moment that we fail to resolve the challenges of the present. . . . We can let ourselves out of such a prison by turning to the Lord for strength. With His help we can use our trials as stepping-stones. The keys are in our hands.

Marvin J. Ashton

SOURCES

Ashton, Marvin J. Quote on p. 9: "If Thou Endure It Well," Oct. 1984 General Conference. Quote on p. 60: Ibid.

Burton, Linda K. 'Is Faith in the Atonement of Jesus Christ Written upon Our Hearts?", Oct. 2012 General Conference.

"Come unto Him." *Hymns,* no. 114. Salt Lake City: The Church of Jesus Christ of Latter-day Saints, 1985.

Covey, Stephen R. in Stephen R. Covey, A. Roger Merrill, Rebecca R. Merrill, *First Things First Every Day: Daily Reflections—Because Where You're Headed Is More Important Than How Fast You Get There* (New York: Simon and Schuster, 1997), 115.

da Vinci, Leonardo. https://www.brainyquote.com/quotes/leonardo_da_vinci_120053?src=t_trouble.

Dibb, Ann M. "I Know It, I Live It, I Love It," Nov. 2012 General Conference.

Edersheim, Alfred. https://www.azquotes.com/quote/925042.

Evans, Richard L. *Thoughts for One Hundred Days: Volume Four* (Salt Lake City: Publishers Press, 1970), 169.

Faust, James E. Quote on pp. 20–21: "Where Do I Make My Stand?", Oct. 2004 General Conference. Quote on p. 49: "The Refiner's Fire," Apr. 1979 General Conference.

Hales, Robert D. "Christian Courage: The Price of Discipleship," Oct. 2008 General Conference.

Hill, Napoleon. https://www.brainyquote.com/quotes/napoleon_hill_121336.

Hinckley, Marjorie Pay. "At Home with the Hinckleys," interview by Marvin K. Gardner and Don A. Searle, *Liahona,* Oct. 2003.

Kapp, Ardeth G. "A Time for Hope," Oct. 1986 General Conference

Keller, Helen. https://www.brainyquote.com/quotes/helen_keller_101340.

Kimball, Heber C. Quoted in "Prophecy of Heber C. Kimball," *Deseret News,* Church Section, May 23, 1931, 3.

Kimball, Spencer W. *The Teachings of Spencer W. Kimball,* ed. Edward L. Kimball (Salt Lake City: Deseret Book Co., 1982), 77.

Landers, Ann. https://www.quotes.net/quote/2186.

Lee, Harold B. Quote on p. 16: Closing Remarks, Oct. 1973 General Conference. Quote on pp. 28–29: "A Sure Trumpet Sound: Quotations from President Lee," *Ensign,* Feb. 1974, 78.

Mandino, Og. *The Greatest Miracle in the World* (New York: Frederick Fell Publishers, 1975), 61.

Maxwell, Neal A. "Encircled in the Arms of His Love," Oct. 2002 General Conference.

Meir, Golda. https://www.brainyquote.com/quotes/golda_meir_121702.

Menlove, Coleen K. "Living Happily Ever After," Apr. 2000 General Conference.

Monson, Thomas S. Quote on p. 1: "God Be with You Till We Meet Again," Oct. 2012 General Conference. Quote on p. 8: "Go for It!", Apr. 1989 General Conference. Quote on p. 25: "'I Will Not Fail Thee, nor Forsake Thee,'" Oct. 2013 general conference. Quote on p. 32: "God Be with You Till We Meet Again," Oct. 2012 General Conference. Quote on p. 59: "The Will Within," Apr. 1987 General Conference.

Moyer, Donna. https://history.churchofjesuschrist.org/media/ac-2009-02-164-wca0864?lang=eng#1.

Oscarson, Bonnie L. "Defy Gravity: Go Forward with Faith," *Liahona*, Aug. 2014.

Packer, Boyd K. Quote on p. 14: "And a Little Child Shall Lead Them," Apr. 2012 General Conference. Quote on p. 34: "Truths Most Worth Knowing," BYU Devotional (Provo, UT), 6 Nov. 2011. Quote on p. 57: "Solving Emotional Problems in the Lord's Own Way," Apr. 1978 General Conference.

Parkin, Bonnie D. "Gratitude: A Path to Happiness," Apr. 2007 General Conference.

Peale, Norman Vincent. *The Positive Principle Today: How to Renew and Sustain the Power of Positive Thinking* (Danbury, CT: Guideposts, 1976).

Peterson, H. Burke. "Adversity and Prayer," Oct. 1973 General Conference.

Reeves, Linda. "Worthy of Our Promised Blessings," Oct. 2015 General Conference.

Schweitzer, Albert. https://www.quotes.net/quote/4110.

Scott, Richard G. Quote on page 23: "The Sustaining Power of Faith in Times of Uncertainty and Testing," Apr. 2003 General Conference. Quote on p. 38: "Learning to Recognize Answers to Prayer," Oct. 1989 General Conference.

Smith, Joseph. *Teachings of the Prophet Joseph Smith*, comp. Joseph Fielding Smith (Salt Lake City: Deseret Book. Co., 1938), 135.

Snow, Eliza R. "The Lord Is My Trust," in Eliza R. Snow, *Poems, Religious, Historical, and Political*, vol. 1 (1856), 148–49.

Stephens, Carole M. "The Master Healer," Oct. 2016 General Conference.

Tanner, Susan W. "All Things Shall Work Together for Your Good," Apr. 2004 General Young Women Meeting.

ten Boom, Corrie. https://www.crosswalk.com/faith/spiritual-life/inspiring-quotes/30-inspiring-christian-quotes.html.

Whitney, Orson F. Quoted by Spencer W. Kimball in *Faith Precedes the Miracle* (Salt Lake City: Deseret Book Co., 1972), 98.

Wilcox, Ella Wheeler. *The Art of Being Alive*. 1914. http://www.ellawheelerwilcox.org/books/artofbeing/2.htm.

Wirthlin, Joseph B. "Come What May, and Love It," Oct. 2008 General Conference.

Young, Brigham. *Discourses of Brigham Young*. sel. John A. Widtsoe (Salt Lake City: Deseret Book Co.,1941), 245.

Ziglar, Zig. https://quotefancy.com/quote/943307/Zig-Ziglar-Difficult-roads-often-lead-to-beautiful-destinations-The-best-is-yet-to-come.